Miracle Reunion

A daughter given up for adoption and
a faith-filled journey to restoration

Peter Cannon

Miracle Reunion

Copyright © 2024 by Dwight Rich and Dennis Bacon
Published by Genesis Press
Visalia, Calif.
www.genesispress.net

Scripture quotations marked (NIV) are taken from the Holy Bible, New International Version®, NIV®. Copyright © 1973, 1978, 1984, 2011 by Biblica, Inc.™ Used by permission of Zondervan. All rights reserved worldwide. www.zondervan.com The "NIV" and "New International Version" are trademarks registered in the United States Patent and Trademark Office by Biblica, Inc.™

Scripture quotations marked (NLT): Scripture quotations are taken from the *Holy Bible*, New Living Translation, copyright © 1996, 2004, 2015 by Tyndale House Foundation. Used by permission of Tyndale House Publishers, Inc., Carol Stream, Illinois 60188. All rights reserved.

Scripture quotations marked (KJV) are taken from the King James Version of the Bible, and are in the public domain.

Cover photos: Jo Anne's college photo, Debbie Bacon at six months old, Dwight's Navy photo. Photo frame courtesy of Shutterstock.com. Photo enhancement courtesy of Face 26 / face26.com / Back cover: Dwight and Jo Anne Rich; Debbie Bacon and Jo Anne.

Text transcribed from audio CD's of presentations by Jo Anne Rich and Debbie Bacon, from an interview with Dwight Rich May 26, 2024, and from various details given by Lisa Bergthold, Debbie Parker and Dennis and Debbie Bacon.

Dedication

This book is dedicated to all those who have lost loved ones—given up for adoption, or those who are adopted and longing to know their birth parents. Hopefully, this story will be an encouragement to them to seek the Lord's perfect will in their lives!

There is no doubt in our minds that the Lord orchestrated this miraculous reunion. We also want to dedicate this book to Him, the only source of lasting joy, peace, and love.

—*Dwight and Family*

Contents

Introduction

Jo Anne Rich, Hume Lake Retreat, 1991

"I have a sweater on the easel up here that a friend and I made a few years back. If you'll notice...the underside of the sweater has a few strings that hang down—it's kind of straggly looking, and it isn't something particularly pretty, but sometimes neither is our lives."

"As we share with you today, the story I'm telling you is not one that is particularly easy to tell because it brings up lots of painful memories. It seems like each time I tell this story, that I live it over again. It's not easy, but it's a story of God's unfailing love, sovereignty and forgiveness."

"Our life is determined by choices—choices that we make. My story is a story about choices that I made as a teen that affected my whole life. As I tell you my story, maybe some of you can relate to some of the things that I've been through. Maybe some of you are adopted. Maybe you are a mother who has given up a child for adoption. Maybe a similar thing has happened to you, and nobody really knows about it. But I think you can see through my life that God did answer my prayer, as it says in Romans 8:28:"

"And we know that all things work together for good to them that love God, to them who are called according to his purpose." (KJV)

Miracle Reunion

1.

Mount Pleasant

Mount Pleasant, Iowa is a classic Midwestern small town in the Southeastern corner of the state about 45 miles from the border with Illinois and Missouri. In the years leading up to and including the Civil War, Mount Pleasant's Opera House hosted abolitionist speakers such as Frederick Douglass and Sojourner Truth. By the 1950's, the village had grown to approximately 6,000 residents. Many of them worked and lived on farms, with grains, soybeans, corn and livestock being the main sources of income. The rest of this Henry County seat's residents ran small businesses and lived in town. One of those was the Shell gasoline station, owned and run by Glen Donald.

Glen was a hard-working man who put in long hours as owner of one of only three service stations in the town. For many years, having no employees, he not only pumped gas, but also fixed flat tires and performed oil changes and lube jobs.

Glen's wife, Margaret, was active in her church, Mount Pleasant Baptist Church, and was a Sunday school superintendent. She was also a homemaker, raising four

1

children—Bill, Bob, Jo Anne and Susie. A half-brother, George, also spent much time with the family in their home.

Beverly Jo Anne Donald was born on November 10, 1934, in Mt. Pleasant, at the very height of the Great Depression. The stock market crash of 1929, along with years of drought, caused many farms to go bankrupt. Unemployment was very high, and many families struggled to make ends meet.

As Jo Anne grew up, she and her family faithfully attended church. Margaret loved God's word and was a faithful prayer warrior. She taught her family the importance of prayer and memorizing scripture. She would often say, "Why worry when you can pray?" Jo Anne realized the importance of these virtues and passed them down to her daughters. Her daughters, in turn, passed these same virtues down to their children. Jo Anne remembers her parents as strict. "We were not allowed to smoke, drink, play cards nor go to movies," Jo Anne recalled years later. "Many times, I was taken out of church and spanked because I did not sit still."

Saved during Sunday school

A positive milestone in her life happened when Jo Anne vividly remembers the day she gave her life to the Lord. "I'll never forget my Sunday school teacher, Rosie Tewalt. One Sunday she asked how many of us would like to go to heaven. Well of course, we all raised our hands. Everybody wanted to go to heaven. Mrs. Tewalt told us that she would tell us how to get there."

Mrs. Tewalt quoted Romans 3:23: *"For all have sinned, and come short of the glory of God."* (KJV) She also quoted John 3:16: *"For God so loved the world, that he gave his only begotten Son, that whosoever believeth in him should not perish, but have everlasting life."* (KJV)

2

"Then she held up a picture of Jesus knocking at a door. She then read to the class Revelation 3:20: *'Behold, I stand at the door, and knock: if any man hear my voice, and open the door, I will come in to him, and will sup with him, and he with me.'* (KJV) Then Mrs. Tewalt asked the class to look at the picture and tell her what we saw different about it."

"We all sat there, squinted our eyes and looked, and pretty soon, one little boy raised his hand and said that there was no handle on the door! And she said that he was right! That handle is not on that door because that door represents your heart! When Christ comes in, he never forces his way in. Only YOU can open that door from within yourself! She went on to tell us that the only way to heaven is to ask Christ into your life."

On that same day, at the age of 12, Jo Anne invited Christ into her heart and was baptized a short time later.

A hot fudge sundae on a T-shirt

After Jo Anne was baptized, life continued, though with occasional bumps in the road. Jo Anne remembers she had a bit of a temper, which could flare up at times. "Just because you accept Christ, things aren't always one hundred percent okay," Jo Anne recalled. "We still have our old sin nature, and mine came out in various ways. I'll never forget the time my brother, Bob, who was three years older than me, came home one day. I was sitting there watching TV—The Lone Ranger—now that kind of dates me. He brought his girlfriend Jo Ann, now his wife, with him."

"He walked in the door, and he asked me what I was watching. After I told him, he thought he would be really smart and impress his girlfriend, and he just went and changed the channel. I got so mad at him, I told him to turn it back! He wouldn't do it, and of course he was

3

bigger than me, so I didn't think there was much that I could do. However, as I was sitting there eating a bowl of ice cream with hot fudge on it, I looked down at the ice cream, and I looked at him. He had a nice white clean T-shirt on, and I went up to him, and I thought I'm going to get you! So, I took that ice cream and I just threw it right on his chest!"

Then, Jo Anne realized that maybe she had gone too far. "I looked at the ice cream dripping on his chest and all over mother's carpet. I looked up at him, and I saw him getting red in the face! I made a beeline for the bathroom door because that was the only door that had a lock on it! As I ran around the corner, I happened to glance over at his girlfriend, Jo Ann, and she had the most horrified look on her face! I knew she was thinking, 'what in the world am I getting myself into?'"

Life on the family farm

Dwight Rich was born December 19, 1935 on the family farm seven miles from Wayland, Iowa to Allen and Alice Rich. Dwight was their fifth child, and he was raised with two older sisters and two older brothers. His mother unexpectedly passed away when he was just 15 months old. Alice had taken a fall on the ice and developed a blood clot. The doctor put her on bed rest for two weeks. After that he told her he thought it would be all right for her to get up. But when she did, the blood clot dislodged and ended up taking her life. This devastated his father, so to lighten the load, Allen's parents moved in to help take care of the children.

For Dwight, life on the farm included chores, such as collecting eggs from the hens and milking cows. As he got older, he helped his father bale hay and drive the tractors. The family grew corn, wheat, oats and soybeans. Besides raising chickens and cows, they raised horses and pigs.

Dwight's family attended the Church of God, a little country church about a mile and a half from the farm. While growing up, Dwight's father insisted that they all go to church every Sunday and Wednesday. When Dwight was 11 years old, he accepted Jesus Christ as his personal savior at one of the services. He was later baptized in a nearby creek. Creek baptisms were a common occurrence at that time. In the early days, they went to church in a horse-driven wagon until Dwight's father bought a Ford Model T.

Dwight recalled hearing his grandfather, Phillip, tell the story of the time when he was 20 years old and bought a brand-new suit with buttons on it. Phillip attended an Amish church, where they practiced the "hook and eye" Amish tradition. They believed that buttons were a form of vanity and were not to be on clothing. When he went to church wearing his new suit, some of the men in the church came to him and cut the buttons off his suit. This hurt Phillip, so he never returned to the church, nor any church for that matter.

Dwight remembered a story that his father shared with him regarding his mother Alice. She had told Allen that if anything ever happened to her that she would want him to marry one of her friends, Mabel Buck. Alice knew Mabel was a strong Christian, and she felt that she could give the children a good home. In 1942, when Dwight was six years old, Allen Rich and Mabel Buck were married. Dwight remembers her taking great care of the family and being a hard worker. She was kind and loving to them all.

From the time Dwight was in kindergarten until the eighth grade, he attended a little one room country school that had only around a dozen children. When Dwight was in the fifth grade, he received a silver dollar for his perfect attendance for the whole year. He was quite proud of that award and still carries the silver dollar with him to this day.

Jo Anne meets Dwight

Jo Anne attended Mount Pleasant High School, beginning in 1949. Her love for music was apparent early on in her life. She loved to sing and was active in her high school choir and sang in many trio and quartet ensembles. She learned to play the piano at an early age and enjoyed playing and singing Gospel hymns, especially in church. Jo Anne also played the trumpet and French horn in her high school marching band. With Jo Anne's playful and outgoing personality, she also participated in cheerleading for the Mount Pleasant Panthers.

In her sophomore year in high school, in 1950, Jo Anne met Dwight Rich, a shy farm boy who lived a few miles outside of town. On the first day of high school, Dwight walked into study hall and sat down. It was a meeting that would change both of their lives forever.

"I'll never forget the first time I met Dwight," Jo Anne recalled. He walked into study hall one day. I was a sophomore, and he was just a freshman. He had a crew cut, very blonde hair and a fair complexion. He sat down right across from me. I would look over at him, and every time he would get really red in the face! I would go back to my friends, and I would say, 'You know there's this goofy kid that sits across from me in study hall, and every time I look at him, he just gets so red in the face!' We made fun of him! Of course, I wrote notes to him to kind of flirt with him. He said they were love notes, but they weren't!"

Dwight recalled his first meeting with Jo Anne vividly. "She started talking with me, and she just embarrassed

6

me. She flirted with me a little bit, and I thought, here was a girl who was older than me and very popular with her classmates. Up to that point, I hadn't had much experience with girls!"

Dwight later became involved in sports at Mount Pleasant High, playing running back and linebacker on the football team. "I loved the roughness of tackling the running backs," he said. He also was on the track team and was the fastest in his high school in the 100-yard dash.

Jo Anne graduated from high school in 1953. Even though she had given her life to the Lord in years past, she felt a type of emptiness inside.

"I went through all the motions of living a Christian life," Jo Anne observed. "I went to youth groups, I memorized Scriptures—I did all that I should have done, but I was doing it for all the wrong reasons. I really think I was doing it for my mom because my mom was the one who really pushed me. There was no real peace nor joy in my life, and I continued to feel this way through high school. In the summer of 1954, before I went to college, I started dating Dwight."

Dating Dwight

Jo Anne and Dwight began dating his senior year in high school. Dwight was "impressed with her because she was a beautiful young lady. I never even imagined that I would date and marry her because she was a year older and graduated a year before I did."

Dwight noted that after Jo Anne's graduation, she stayed in town and worked. One day, Dwight was with his cousin at a restaurant in Mount Pleasant named the "Candy Kitchen." Jo Anne, always the friendly, outgoing one, walked up to the two and said, "Can I sit in this booth with you?"

Dwight replied, "Sure!" Afterwards, Dwight playfully accused Jo Anne of "picking up" on him.

Jo Anne indicated a young man sitting a few booths over. "I don't want to sit by that guy over there." So, she sat in the booth with Dwight and his cousin. After they were done, Dwight asked Jo Anne, "Do you want a ride home?" Jo Anne said, "Yes," and according to Dwight, "It was the first time we actually did anything, other than just in school."

Dwight recalls what they did that last summer before Jo Anne left for college. "We would go to the drive-in theater." He liked western movies, but Jo Anne didn't, so they would choose something else. In high school, they would also have dances at the student union, with music played on a record player. "We didn't dance," Dwight said. "She didn't like to dance, and I didn't either, but we'd go there and visit with the other high school students."

Off to college

In the fall of 1954, Jo Anne said good-bye to her parents and friends. Dwight drove her in his 1953 Ford sedan about 850 miles to Bob Jones College in Greenville, South Carolina. Dwight remembered that Jo Anne's mother wanted her to go there because it was such a conservative college.

The college, now Bob Jones University, was founded in 1927 by Christian evangelist Bob Jones. Jones was a friend of William Jennings Bryan, a former congressman, presidential candidate and secretary of state under President Woodrow Wilson. Bryan was a staunch Christian who at one point was the lead prosecuting attorney in the famous Scopes Trial in 1925. This was when high school teacher, John T. Scopes, was accused of violating Tennessee's Butler Act, which had made it illegal for teachers to teach human evolution in any state-funded school.[1]

Jones recalled that in 1924, his friend Bryan, had leaned over to him at a Bible conference service in Winona Lake, Indiana and said, "If schools and colleges do not quit teaching evolution as a fact, we are going to become a nation of atheists." [2]

So, sometime later, Jones founded the college named after him. Bob Jones University had a reputation for having some of the most rigid rules of any in higher education, as Jo Anne vividly remembers.

"You couldn't go to a stricter school! I got there and here I was a freshman, all excited and...looking forward to meeting new people and going on outings. We found out that if you went out with a boy, you had to have a chaperone everywhere you went! Then I found out that even MARRIED couples could not hold hands on campus because it was a "bad influence" on those of us who were not married! They caught one couple kissing in the broom closet, and they kicked them out of school!"

"The worst thing of all was their food! It was just awful!" Jo Anne complained. "I'll never forget the first time I went to breakfast because they had grits, gravy, corn pone and black-eyed peas! Doesn't that sound awful? I lived on macaroni and cheese and bread because I just could not eat anything else!"

Fortunately, Jo Anne did love her music classes and was starting to make friends with several students.

Unexpected news

However, within a few months after Jo Anne arrived at the college, she started feeling sick, and it wasn't the

---

[1] "Tennessee Anti-evolution Statute—UMKC School of Law." Umkc.edu. Archived from the original on May 20, 2009.

[2] "Standing Without Apology: The History of Bob Jones University" by Daniel L. Turner, p. 9

food she was eating.

"I didn't have any idea what was wrong. I thought I had the flu. Well, I went to the doctor after I did not get any better. I was throwing up all three meals."

After running some tests, the doctor said he didn't find anything in her blood work but that he wanted to run one more test.

"When he came in, he had a very stern look on his face," Jo Anne remembered.

The doctor said, "I'm sorry to tell you, but you are pregnant."

"I thought my heart would break. I was petrified! I turned my face to the wall, and I cried bitter tears," Jo Anne recalled. "I knew my whole education was going down the drain and that I would be expelled from school. I was scared. I didn't know what to do. I didn't know what my friends would say. I didn't know what my folks would say. I cried, and I cried."

The doctor notified the dean of women at the university, who told Jo Anne to go to her room and to stay there.

The dean said, "You are not to come out for meals. Your meals will be sent to you. We're going to send for your parents, and I don't want you to come out until they get here."

So, Jo Anne was forced to stay in her room for a day and a half, with no contact with her roommates. In fact, her roommates had moved out because "they didn't want anything to do with me, and they felt ashamed," Jo Anne observed.

"I was numb. I was so confused. I had a lot of time to sit, think and cry," Jo Anne said, "but I began to pray for the first time because I knew I had really made a mess of my life."

Jo Anne's parents, along with her pastor from church,

arrived and picked her up. Jo Anne said, "I dreaded getting into the car with my mother because I didn't know what in the world she was going to say to me. But she did something that I'll never, ever forget. She reached over, and she took my hand, and she held it all the way home." On the journey home they discussed her future. Jo Anne remembered, "Not once did my parents put me down. They did not tell me how terrible I was."

At one point, her father asked her, "Jo Anne, do you want to marry Dwight?"

Jo Anne replied, "Oh, Dad, I don't know. I'm so scared and so mixed up. Two wrongs don't make a right, just because I'm pregnant!" She pointed out that Dwight was not living out his Christian faith and that getting married would just make things worse. Jo Anne added, "I don't know what to do—I don't think I can marry him."

After a very difficult and emotional discussion, it was decided to put the baby up for adoption. Her parents agreed with her that this would be the best course of action. In addition, they all agreed not to tell Dwight where she would be staying nor about the pregnancy.

Booth Memorial Hospital

The pastor made arrangements for Jo Anne to stay at a home for unwed mothers at the Booth Memorial Hospital in Chicago, operated by the Salvation Army. It was named after the Salvation Army's founder, Methodist minister William Booth. Back in the 1950's, and even before, pregnant unmarried women had very few places to go. Families of such young ladies were shocked and embarrassed by the stigma of out-of-wedlock births, which could cause repercussions in both their churches and communities.

So, in the late 1800's and all through the 1900's, organizations such as the Salvation Army built hospitals to meet the needs of the poor. That included mothers with babies born out-of-wedlock. There were also Booth hospitals in New York City, Cleveland, Detroit and other cities. After the Donald family returned to Mount Pleasant, Jo Anne stayed at her brother Bob's house while the pastor finished up arrangements for Jo Anne to go to the Booth hospital.

"Getting pregnant in those days was nothing like it is today," Jo Anne observed decades later. "Today it's a little more accepted. You can go to school pregnant. You can keep your child. Many schools have daycares where the child can go while the mom continues her studies. You can take birthing classes. There are so many more opportunities, and people don't look down on you. But back then, it was terrible. It was not accepted at all. It was very difficult. We pregnant girls, would go into restaurants, and we would have a hard time getting waited on. As we would walk down the streets, people would call out terrible things to us."

Meanwhile, Dwight was not told of her pregnancy by Jo Anne's parents nor the pastor. "I didn't even have a chance to talk to her nor see her," Dwight said later.

Mr. and Mrs. Donald drove Jo Anne to the Booth Hospital, which included living facilities for the soon-to-be mothers.

A dorm full of pregnant girls

"It was quite a large dorm," Jo Anne remembered. "There were 150 pregnant girls. I did not fit in—I didn't have anything in common with them, as I grew up in a very sheltered home. They were quite different. It was a very lonely time. I made one friend who taught me how to knit. I'm very grateful for her to this day. I had one nurse who also befriended me."

Jo Anne was put to work. "My job was to scrub floors,"

Jo Anne recalled. "I scrubbed floors eight hours a day. I was also very sick. I had morning, noon and evening sickness. I would scrub floors, and then I would go over to the sink and throw up. I did that all day long."

During this time of isolation from her family, in the midst of an unfamiliar environment, Jo Anne began to really seek the Lord for the first time in a long time, spending much time in prayer. She was especially overcome with a desire to totally commit her life to God after hearing a radio broadcast. One night, she was sitting in the dining room where the radio was located.

"I was switching stations on the radio looking for something to listen to," Jo Anne recalled. "All of a sudden I heard this very familiar voice. It was Theodore Epp from the *Back to the Bible* broadcast."

Epp was a well-known Christian evangelist whose radio program ran from 1939 to 1985, eventually syndicated on more than 800 radio stations worldwide.[3]

Jo Anne's prayer

The broadcast brought back memories for Jo Anne of her mother listening to Epp on a daily basis. This time, the message touched Jo Anne's heart.

He said, "How many of you listening to the sound of my voice have no peace, no joy, are going through the motions of living a Christian life but...Christ is not the Lord of your life?"

Jo Anne felt he was speaking to her. She got down on her knees to pray, and remembered a Bible verse:

"If we confess our sins, he is faithful and just to forgive us our sins, and to cleanse us from all unrighteousness." (1 John 1:9 KJV)

---

[3] "700 Famous Nebraskans." Nebraska Press Association. 2006. Archived from the original on 2006-11-14. Retrieved 2008-06-04

"With tears streaming down my face," Jo Anne said, "I got down on my knees, right beside that chair, and I asked God to forgive me for what I had done. I asked Him to come in and become Lord of my life."

After claiming that verse and a time of prayer, Jo Anne said, "God did forgive me that day. He gave me a peaceful feeling knowing for the first time that Christ was Lord of my life. I was going to turn around and make things different. I was going to live for Him."

During those months at the Booth facility, Jo Anne's parents came for her one time—at Christmas. By this time, Jo Anne was about four months pregnant. They drove her back to Mt. Pleasant, but she was not allowed to speak to anyone about her pregnancy. Her dad took Jo Anne to a high school basketball game, but Dwight remembers that "Jo Anne would not speak to me that night. Later on I realized why she was so uncomfortable talking to me."

Jo Anne gives birth

After Christmas, Jo Anne was driven back to Chicago. In the months that followed, Jo Anne's bouts of sickness associated with the pregnancy continued. The day of the birth, Jo Anne went into labor for about 19 hours. There was no anesthetic of any kind because it was not available, according to Jo Anne. Another challenge was that Jo Anne's doctor was from Germany and spoke little English.

A baby girl was born to Jo Anne on April 23, 1955. Jo Anne named her "Rebecca." The nurses asked her if she would like to see and hold the baby.

Jo Anne replied, "I think I would like to see her, but I don't dare hold her because I don't know if I could give her up!" Jo Anne walked to the nursery, stood in the doorway, and looked inside. A nurse held up the baby for her to see, and "there was this little blond-haired, blue-eyed baby! I looked at her, and I knew within my heart that I would probably never see her again!"

Violet, the social worker

Jo Anne left that same day to live in the house of a social worker, whom we shall refer to as "Violet." She stayed there for a few months, until summer vacation, or else the people in Mt. Pleasant would possibly find out where she had been. Jo Anne said this was necessary because she came from a very small town, and her parents did not want others to know of her pregnancy and birth.

Jo Anne remembers Violet as "not a very warm person. In fact, she was pretty strict. She was an old maid, who had never married." Jo Anne recalls Violet would go to church on Sunday morning, and "I would stay at home. I don't know why she didn't take me. Maybe she didn't want to have to explain who I was and why I was there."

In trouble for playing the piano

Jo Anne had been there a short while when another social worker, a man in his 30's who worked with Violet, came to live at the home. He found out that Jo Anne played the piano, so one day, he asked Jo Anne, "Why don't you come out and play the piano with me?"

Jo Anne refused, choosing instead to spend most of her time in her room, trying to adjust to her new life. "I was really depressed," she recalled, "because I was just struggling with my situation."

The social worker kept insisting, and finally, Jo Anne emerged from her room and began playing a duet with the young man. Jo Anne's spirits started to turn positive. "We were laughing and having a good time, and all of a sudden the door opened, and in walked Violet! She had this funny look on her face. She looked at him, and she looked back at me, and said, "What are you doing?" I said, "Well, not anything, really. We're just playing the piano."

Violet shouted, "Get up and go to your room!"

Jo Anne replied, "Why? What have I done?"

Violet simply repeated icily, "Just go to your room!"

Jo Anne got up from the piano bench and headed for her room, wondering what she had done wrong. Violet followed her to her room and told her, "There'll be no supper for you tonight!" Violet said she would speak to her later about this.

Sent to her room without dinner

Jo Anne stayed in her room all night and was denied dinner. She didn't sleep well "because I wondered what in the world was she going to say to me." In the morning Violet walked into her room and said, "I'll be so glad when you're gone from my home because you know, you really are a bad girl!"

"It was like someone taking a knife and stabbing me," Jo Anne felt. "It hurt so bad. To this day, I struggle with my self-esteem. Words that are said can never be taken back."

Years later, speaking before a group, Jo Anne reflected on this incident. "When someone is hurting, they need words of encouragement, rather than words of discouragement and judgment. They don't need a lecture. They simply need kindness and gentleness, just as God has shown his mercy to us. We need to show it to others. I don't know if there are any teenagers here, but if there are, I hope you would not have to learn as I did the hard way. If it does happen to you, I would encourage you to keep the doors open to your parents. Keep communications open. Mom, your response to a situation like this should be in love."

Jo Anne recalls her own mother's response to the news of her pregnancy. "Not one word did she condemn me with. She did not speak harshly to me. I was so grateful for that because I was hard enough on myself. It's important that mothers don't say anything negative with everything that's going through their heads at the time—like, 'Oh, how could you do this to me?' or 'What a disgrace!' or 'What are my friends going to think?' Jo Anne noted that the Bible tells us:

"Wherefore, my beloved brethren, let every man be swift to hear, slow to speak, slow to wrath." (James 1:19 KJV)

Jo Anne concluded, "Remember, whatever you say, she will remember it for the rest of her life. Take a day at a time, pray for wisdom and guidance, and don't look too far in advance, or you'll be consumed by anxiety."

2.

From Iowa to California

It was now June, two months after the birth, and Jo Anne was fully recovered and more than ready to return to Mt. Pleasant. Her parents made the four-hour drive from her hometown and picked her up from Violet's house. Within a week after she returned home, she was walking down the street of the small town, and she met Dwight.

He was totally unaware of Jo Anne's pregnancy and subsequent birth. He thought Jo Anne was still attending Bob Jones College. He asked her how school was going. Jo Anne felt very uncomfortable during their conversation. Then Dwight asked her if she'd like to go out to see a movie.

Jo Anne replied, "No, I don't think so."

Dwight replied, "Oh, come on!"

Jo Anne suddenly got an inspiration and invited him to a revival meeting going on at her church. She thought he wouldn't want to go, but his response surprised her when he said, "I WILL go!" So, they made plans for him to pick her up that night.

A traveling evangelist was preaching at the service, and that same night Dwight walked down the aisle and

18

re-committed his life to the Lord. "I had accepted the Lord as a youngster," Dwight said many years later. "But I certainly wasn't living a Christian life at the time. It was a re-commitment." So Dwight joined Jo Anne each night for the rest of the revival which went on for several days.

Dwight learns of his daughter

At the end of that week, Jo Anne told Dwight she needed to talk to him. She told him what had happened— the pregnancy, the baby girl, everything. Dwight was overcome with emotion upon hearing the news for the first time.

"I was completely flabbergasted," Dwight recalled. "I couldn't believe that she hadn't told me. If she would have, I would have married her because I actually fell in love with her soon after we started dating."

"This was difficult for him," Jo Anne remembers. "I had never seen Dwight cry, and I have never seen him cry like that since."

When Dwight asked Jo Anne why she hadn't told him, she said, "Her mother didn't want anybody in town to know she was pregnant," according to Dwight. "Her mom was a mighty fine person. I never held any grudges against her. I just accepted the fact. That's the way it worked."

Jo Anne recalled that Dwight said, "I have loved you the whole time you were gone, and I want to marry you. I want to see if we can get our baby back."

Jo Anne and Dwight agreed to get married. Dwight had recently enlisted in the Navy and was scheduled to leave in September. Since they didn't have much time before his report date, they decided on a July wedding. They also decided to try and get Rebecca back. They traveled to another town to make a phone call to Chicago because in Mt. Pleasant, they were worried someone like a switchboard operator might be listening in on the conversation and that the gossip would spread like wildfire in the small town.

Dwight recalled, "I knew the situation...her mom was so strong of a Christian that she didn't want anybody in town knowing that Jo Anne had gotten pregnant. That's why all of this transpired."

When Jo Anne called to see if she and Dwight could get Rebecca back, "The person that I had to talk to was Violet," Jo Anne remarked. Jo Anne told Violet that she and Dwight were going to get married, and they wanted their baby back.

Violet replied, "There is no way you're getting your baby back! She's gone! You're not going to see her ever again!" Later on, Jo Anne and Dwight learned that at that point in time, the baby was not gone, and that she had not even been adopted yet.

"But we knew that God had other plans for her," Jo Anne later said. "I accepted that, and I didn't hold anger in my heart because I knew that God had a plan, and I was not to question it."

Marriage and family

Jo Anne and Dwight were married on July 20, 1955 at Jo Anne's home church in Mt. Pleasant. Just a few months later, Dwight reported to the Navy. Dwight had joined the Navy Reserve in high school and attended monthly meetings. So, in September 1955, Dwight reported for active duty. He was assigned to a ship in San Diego, California. As a clerk-typist, his responsibilities were typing, issuing liberty cards, transfer papers and other paperwork.

Jo Anne stayed with her parents for a few weeks until Dwight could make arrangements for her to join him.

"The ship was home ported...and we were remodeling it," Dwight said. "It wasn't going to sea for a long time," so after a few weeks, Jo Anne was able to join her husband.

San Diego to Japan, then back to Iowa

Dwight and Jo Anne got an apartment in San Diego. Jo Anne got hired to work at a bank in the downtown area, while Dwight commuted back and forth from the ship. After six months however, Dwight's ship was ordered to sail for Japan, and Dwight had to leave his newlywed wife. Jo Anne returned to Mt. Pleasant.

After several months, Dwight arranged for Jo Anne to fly to Japan to join him again. "We did all of this by mail—no phones back then!" Of course, there were phones for landline calls, but international calls between countries were difficult or impossible in many circumstances.

It was while Jo Anne was living in Japan when she became pregnant with their daughter, Debbie. Months later, Jo Anne returned to Mt. Pleasant. Afterwards, Dwight was able to leave active duty and return to reserve status which enabled him to return in time for the birth of their daughter.

Debbie was born in 1957 in Burlington, Iowa. Jo Anne chose a doctor in Burlington because she wasn't comfortable with a doctor in Mt. Pleasant knowing that she had already had another child. Their first home was a single wide mobile home in Mt. Pleasant. In 1959, the family moved to Burlington, Iowa.

Dwight got a job with International Resistance Company, which specialized in resistor technology. Dwight enrolled in Burlington Junior College and played football for one year. In 1961, Dwight and Jo Anne were blessed with another daughter, Lisa.

A move to the West

Both of Jo Anne's brothers, Bill and Bob, had moved to Visalia, California with their families. They were both teachers and had gotten jobs with the Visalia Unified School District. Shortly after Jo Anne's brothers relocated, Jo Anne's parents also moved to California. For many years, Margaret had wanted to move to California for the exceptional weather and beautiful countryside. They chose the city of Santa Ana, which is 30 miles south of Los Angeles.

About a year later, Dwight and Jo Anne left Burlington and also made the move to Santa Ana. They stayed with the Donald's until they were able to purchase a home.

A year went by, and Dwight and Jo Anne decided to visit her brothers in Visalia. They all went to church together at First Baptist Church. Dwight recalls, "We went to a Sunday school taught by Jim Farley. I really liked his teaching style and enjoyed listening to him." Dwight learned that Jim worked for the local school district and that he was looking to employ an assistant in the purchasing department.

Dwight said, "I called Mr. Farley regarding the job, and he invited me to his house for an interview. Farley also invited the school district's superintendent. The interview lasted 20 minutes, and they asked me if I could come to work tomorrow." Dwight replied, "I can't do that, but I'll tell you what...I will be here two weeks from tomorrow!"

Dwight and Jo Anne went back to Santa Ana and put their house up for sale. Their house sold in two weeks! Dwight marveled at how God helped him and Jo Anne so many times over the years. "This is how the Lord has worked in our lives!" he said. "It's just amazing how the Lord has everything under his control."

Dwight and Jo Anne became involved in Bible studies

in their church, First Baptist in Visalia. Dwight continued working as the purchasing agent for the Visalia Unified School District, while Jo Anne worked a variety of jobs, one being a music teacher and another as a teller at a local bank. At church, Jo Anne loved music and sang in duets, trios and choir. But despite all her accomplishments, there was one Bible verse in particular Jo Anne found challenging:

"Delight thyself also in the Lord: and he shall give thee the desires of thine heart." (Psalm 37:4 KJV).

As Jo Anne continued to grow in her Christian walk, there was still one desire of her heart she continued to pray for. "I began to meditate on his word and to get into fellowship with Christians and really began to grow in the Lord," she said. "But my one prayer as I prayed through all of these years was that Rebecca would come to know the Lord as her savior. That's all I asked of the Lord because I knew I would never see her." Another verse Jo Anne remembers vividly from that time in her life was Psalm 42:1:

"As the deer pants for streams of water, so my soul pants for you, my God."(NIV)

The Missing Piece
The years passed by, and by the mid-1980's, Dwight and Jo Anne's two daughters were now grown up. Their daughter, Lisa, was living in Reedley, California, 40 miles from Jo Anne and Dwight in Visalia. In 1986, Lisa attended a women's luncheon at a Mennonite church in Reedley, California, and the speaker was Lee Ezell, author of the book, *The Missing Piece.* The book details Lee's life, an unplanned pregnancy, a child given up for

adoption and their reunification years later. After hearing Lee Ezell speak, Lisa was very moved by the story she told and how God's unfailing and unconditional love impacted Lee's life. Lisa shared with Jo Anne how Lee's story impacted her, and Lisa encouraged her mom to buy the book.

But Jo Anne was still carrying the secret of Rebecca's birth through the years and never told her two daughters they had a sister. "It was something you kept a secret," Jo Anne said later. "Something you were ashamed of, so we did not tell them."

But Lisa was persistent. JoAnne said, "I couldn't tell her why, and she just kept bugging me, so I finally said, Lisa, if you want to read the book, I'll buy it and I'll give it to you, but I don't have any desire to read it. Well, I know she thought in her mind, 'what in the world' because we used to exchange books and read them all the time."

Finally, Jo Anne did buy the book, but she gave it to Lisa and said, "Here, you take the book and YOU read it!"

Lisa said later, "I was so perplexed as to why she hadn't read it because she loved to read."

Later, mother and daughter drove to Santa Barbara, California, to pick up Lisa's husband, Derek, who had joined his brother Kurt to work on Kurt's house. During the trip, Lisa told her mother about part of the story of *The Missing Piece,* and she began to cry. Lisa said, "Mom, I don't know why I'm telling you, but I want you to read this book!"

Jo Anne said she thought, "What is this kid up to? Why is she doing this?" So that same day, Lisa gave her mother, *The Missing Piece.*

"It was such an amazing and incredible book," Lisa recalled. "Here was this 20-year-old daughter, given up for adoption, witnessing to her birth mother. I was just marveling how God's hand was amid the whole situation."

On the shelf, then off

When Jo Anne got home, she stuck the book on the bookshelf and didn't read it. Finally, sometime later, she did pull it off the shelf.

"When I sat down to read it, it was just like a dam breaking!" Jo Anne reflected. "I read that book from cover to cover. I began to cry and sob and all the feelings and all the hurts that I had hidden began to pour out."

She continued, "I remember asking the Lord to forgive me for all the hard feelings I had toward that social worker. I asked Him to take control. I had not even considered looking for Rebecca. I just kept it in my heart. I had no one to share it with." She did tell Dwight, but apart from him, she told nobody else.

Jo Anne said after finishing the book, she bowed her head and asked the Lord, "What do I do?" But she continued to keep her secret to herself.

Jo Anne shares her story

Afterwards, Jo Anne and a friend, Cindy, the wife of her church's youth pastor, attended a retreat at Hume Lake in the mountains above Fresno, California. Jo Anne had not told anyone that she had read the book, *The Missing Piece*. "I just kept all these things in my head because I didn't know who to tell," Jo Anne recollected.

After the final service, Jo Anne and Cindy were sitting in her car, waiting for it to stop raining, so they could drive back home. "All of a sudden, I just blurted my story out to Cindy because I felt I needed to tell somebody." After Jo Anne finished sharing, Cindy asked her, "Jo Anne, did you ever think of looking for her?"

Jo Anne replied, "No! I wouldn't even know how to begin!"

Cindy suggested, "Well, why don't you let me help you?"

So later on, the two of them sat down together and wrote a letter to the Salvation Army in Chicago, asking for Jo Anne's baby's birth record for April 23, 1955. But before sending the letter, they prayed, and a Bible verse came to Jo Anne:

"Thou wilt keep him in perfect peace, him whose mind is stayed on thee: because he trusteth in thee." (Isaiah 26:3 KJV).

Jo Anne prayed, "Lord, I cannot go through this chance of rejection, unless You are in the center of this, and I have Your peace." After praying, Jo Anne said, "The Lord really answered my prayer, for on that day I had perfect peace in my heart. We sat down, called the social worker, and she said, 'The first thing you need to do is sit down and tell your girls.'"

For Jo Anne, this was difficult because "I didn't know how they would react." She thought that one of her daughters would take it better than the other. Jo Anne thought Lisa would be the one that would really take it hard. But when Jo Anne finally revealed the two sisters had an adopted sister, it was Debbie who took it the hardest. Debbie said she "wished her parents would have been more open and told us early on. Knowing that my parents had struggles and made some mistakes could have improved our communication, especially in the teen years."

Debbie Parker spoke of her reaction when she learned of her long-lost sister. "I was totally surprised! We were at a family picnic, and my mother pulled me to the side and told me she needed to talk to me. Due to her tone of voice, I immediately thought that someone in the family had a serious health issue. She reassured me that was not the case. She then proceeded to tell me that I have another full-blooded sister!"

Lisa said that after her mother read *The Missing Piece,* she decided "she wanted to look for the baby she had given up for adoption. After she told me, I remember being super excited about it! I couldn't believe that I had another full-blooded sister!" Jo Anne later said if she had everything to do over again that she would have been more transparent with her daughters.

After Jo Anne contacted the adoption agency, they waited to hear if there was any news about Rebecca. In July 1987, a letter arrived saying they did not anticipate it would be difficult to find her. At the end of the month, Jo Anne received another letter.

The letter stated the adopted girl and her parents are aware of the increase of adopted children and reunions with birth parents, but this is something they were not especially interested in pursuing. However, in the letter, it did mention that the adopted girl is a lovely young Christian woman with a husband and a family.

Jo Anne rejoiced upon learning of this news. "I knew God had answered my prayer! I said, okay Lord, if I don't see her here on earth, I'm going to meet her in heaven! I was content, and I just let it go."

3.

A Turning Point

Two and a half years passed by. At this time, Lisa and Derek were now staying with Jo Anne and Dwight, while they were looking to find an apartment. In March 1990, Jo Anne returned from work, and Lisa met her at the door.

"She had a little twinkle in her eye," Jo Anne recalls. "She said, Mom, there's a letter waiting for you on the counter." Lisa had tears in her eyes as Jo Anne picked up the letter, which had been opened. Trembling with anticipation, Jo Anne pulled the letter out of the opened envelope, asking Lisa, "Do you know what's in this letter?"

Lisa replied, "Yeah! Dad and I read it!"

The very first paragraph stated, "The daughter you placed for adoption in 1955 is interested in having some contact with you." "I could hardly read the rest of the letter because I was crying so hard!" Jo Anne remembered.

The last paragraph said, "It will be of interest to

you…that it was Lee Ezell's book, *The Missing Piece,* which prompted your daughter to write to us." The letter included instructions for Jo Anne to write a letter to her, to be forwarded by the adoption agency, and was told they would send it to her long-lost daughter.

Jo Anne was thrilled, but also wondered, "Now how do you sit down and write a letter about what has transpired for 35 years and tell it all in one letter?" So, she prayed and felt "the Lord really gave me the words." Then, at the end of the letter she closed with, "Love, your Extended Family." She also included her name, address, and phone number. Shortly afterwards, she received another letter saying that the adoption agency had forwarded Jo Anne's letter but without the identifying information.

A letter from Debbie

To Jo Anne's surprise, enclosed with the letter was *another* letter. Jo Anne opened it up, and there across the top of the stationary were three hearts and a duck inside the middle heart. Jo Anne was amazed! "If you have ever been in my home, I have 13 or 14 ducks because I LOVE ducks! I have duck pictures, I have ducks on my hearth, I have ducks everywhere!"

Jo Anne eagerly read the letter, which began, "Hi, my name is Debbie, and I am the daughter that you gave up for adoption 34 years ago." Jo Anne was shocked to hear that Rebecca had been renamed, Debbie, by her adopted parents. The letter went on to say that her husband's name was Dennis. In an amazing coincidence, Jo Anne and Dwight's other daughter, Debbie Parker, ALSO has a husband named Dennis! (Though he goes by his middle name Alan). "So now," Jo Anne laughed, "We have two Debbie's and two Dennis's!" Dwight's response was "Boy, does the Lord have a sense of humor!"

The letter further revealed that Debbie, the adopted daughter, was a pediatric intensive care nurse, that her husband was a policeman, and that she had four children! Jo Anne noted that with this news, they now had nine grandchildren!

Later on, Dwight and Jo Anne were discussing this news, and Jo Anne was bursting with excitement. "Dwight, do you think we would be able to go back to Chicago to see Debbie?"

Dwight replied, "You bet we will! We'll figure out some way to get there!"

A few days later, Jo Anne returned from choir practice on a Wednesday evening. Dwight, Lisa and Derek were quietly talking. As soon as Jo Anne walked into the room, Dwight, his voice quivering in anticipation and indicating a note, said, "Jo Anne, you're to call this number."

Jo Anne picked up the note and noticed the name, Debbie Bacon, San Jose! Jo Anne looked up at Dwight, puzzled. "Who's Debbie Bacon?" she asked.

Dwight excitedly replied, "That is our birth daughter!"

Jo Anne looked at the note again, then said, "San Jose?"

Dwight replied, "Yes! She called just a little while ago, and I talked to her. She wants you to call her!"

Jo Anne headed for the back bedroom to make a private call, but Dwight said, "Oh, no! You're not going to do that because Lisa and Derek sat and listened to MY conversation! So, WE'RE going to listen to YOURS!"

So, Jo Anne dialed the number, and spoke to her daughter, Debbie, for the first time in her life.

"We both had plenty to say," Jo Anne remembered. "We found out her dad was a youth pastor. We had many similarities. She's nearsighted and wears contacts. We all wear contacts or glasses. We both have the same blood type. We both sing alto in the choir. Then she made a very interesting statement. She said, "Jo Anne, I was placed in my parents' home the day that you and Dwight got married!" Jo Anne recalled the phone call she made to Violet, the social worker, years ago. She and Dwight now realized that their baby hadn't even been adopted yet as they had been told.

Debbie mentioned that her adoptive parents were having a hard time accepting her contacting her birth parents. So, mother and daughter, separated after 34 years, both prayed together for the first time. They asked the Lord to intercede on Debbie's adoptive parents' behalf, to soften their hearts and give them peace concerning this miracle reunion.

4.

Debbie's Story

As Jo Anne listened in amazement at all the wonderful details Debbie described over the phone, and those she learned later on, she and Debbie both marveled at the way the Lord had moved to bring them both together after all these years.

In that women's conference at Hume Lake described earlier, along with other talks, both Jo Anne and Debbie shared their incredible story with those in attendance. After Jo Anne had presented her side of the story, Debbie filled in the missing parts of the story.

Debbie's childhood

Debbie shared, "I was adopted by a wonderful Christian couple in the Chicago area." Debbie's adoptive father was Gunnar Hoglund, a Baptist minister and youth director for the Baptist General Conference in Chicago, Illinois.

He was the leader of a youth outreach called "Hi-C". Her mother, Doris, was a student and was active in the program. Doris was a stunning co-ed beauty. Debbie was sure she caught her father's eye during the sessions. Debbie went on to share, "I am certain she was equally enthralled by the six-foot-one Swedish preacher with a deep compelling voice. They dated for a while and were eventually married in 1952."

Debbie's mother had grown up in the church pastored by A. W. Tozer. Pastor Tozer later went on from preaching and shepherding at his church to become a well-known Christian author. Pastor Tozer had a special fondness for Doris and agreed to officiate their wedding vows. It was not long after being married they found they could not have children. The disappointment was overwhelming. They both had wanted a family and were anxious to fill their home with children.

Debbie's adoption

God soon led them to seek adoption. The process even then was a grueling amount of paperwork, interviews and waiting. They relied on God's timing and patiently awaited their turn. The foster care mother who attended to children before adoption had taken a special liking to Gunnar and "Dorie," as those close to her referred to her. They had developed a special friendship during the waiting process. The foster care mother promised to keep an eye out for the perfect fit for their family. After what seemed an eternity, the adoption agency eventually called.

Debbie later commented she was sure they were "sitting on pins and needles during that call." The agency let them know a little girl had just become available for adoption. The agency indicated this little one might be the perfect fit for their home. Dorie and Gunnar hurried to the agency. They were greeted by the foster care giver and a tiny little blonde-haired baby.

After one visit, they agreed this little baby would be

the perfect fit for their home. On July 20th, 1955, Debbie's new parents brought her home to live with them. She was just three months old.

Youth camps, travel and home life

Debbie's father Gunnar continued to work in the Midwest area. For the first 15 years of her life, Gunnar did not pastor in a church. He continued working out of the Baptist General Conference headquarters.

Because of his position, he traveled as a participant in multiple international youth crusades. Those included trips to Germany, Ethiopia, Switzerland, Australia and U.S. Youth Crusades with the Reverend Billy Graham. Debbie went on to share, "While my brother and I did not travel with him internationally, we did a lot of traveling throughout the United States."

"We attended various youth camps and conferences where my dad would be the speaker. I have a lot of very happy, warm memories of my childhood, just traveling from place to place. We traveled to just about every state in the country. We soon became the spoiled brats of the camp because our dad was the speaker. It was a lot of fun!"

Debbie recalled, "Our home was a very godly home, one where we were taught from a very early age who God was, to follow Him always and what He could do for you in your life. I was about five years old when my mother, Doris, prayed with me and helped lead me to the Lord."

Debbie was aware of her adoption from an early age. "My parents were always very open about the fact that my brother, Jeff, who was two years younger than me, and I had been adopted. We knew how desperately they had wanted children. There was never any doubt in either my mind, or in my brother's mind, that our parents loved us very much. We both knew we had a very special place in their home and that God had chosen them for us."

Questions about being adopted

Despite knowing she as adopted, Debbie didn't always feel comfortable about being a bit different from her friends. Her father had written several articles for the conference magazine and various newsletters affiliated with the church denomination. One of those articles was about the adoption of Debbie and Jeff. Debbie shared, "If it ever was a secret we were adopted, that secret was no more; everybody knew. Everyone knowing just added to my embarrassment and discomfort. Looking back, I know how silly it was to have those thoughts."

"For a high school writing assignment, I once wrote a short story about my adoption," Debbie recalled. "I spent little time in questioning why I was given up and considerable time on the merits of adoption and how lucky I had been. My Dad appreciated my insights. The article was later published in the monthly newsletter of the Baptist General Conference. Despite telling my story, I still felt awkward about being different than my friends and others at school."

Debbie remembered thinking from a very young age, "I wish I was just like my friends. I would hate it when people would come up and say to me, 'Boy, you don't look like your brother at all!' Or, 'Where did you come from? You don't look like your parents at all!' It would always make me feel a bit embarrassed. I would simply share that I was adopted."

As Debbie grew older, she found that going to the doctor would always be a very traumatic time for her. During the exam the doctor would get around to asking questions about her medical history. Debbie would tell him, "I don't know the answer to that," and explain that

"I was adopted." After becoming a nurse, Debbie realized that knowing detailed information about her family health history became more and more important to her.

A lone link on a chain

Debbie continued, "I guess if I were to try and explain some more of my feelings about what it felt like to be adopted, I've made a little analogy here. I hope this will help you understand a little bit better for those of you who are not adopted. I would look at my friends around me who came from conventional kinds of families. They were able to explain where they got that natural curly hair or where that funny little personality quirk came from or say things like 'that's something Aunt So-and-So used to do.'"

"I looked at them and knew they had their own personal link on a long chain of people that had come before them, a link of generation after generation after generation. That missing part of me helped add to feeling a bit isolated. It was like a lone link on a chain that just didn't have any connection to the past. It was a lonely feeling despite all the support I had from my parents."

Debbie recalled that from a very young age she did not ask a lot of questions about her adoption or the circumstances of her birth. "My brother and I could tell that those kinds of questions made Mom and Dad feel uncomfortable. The last thing we wanted to do was hurt them. As a result, I learned to keep quiet and not broach the subject."

Debbie did remember asking her parents, "Why did my birth parents give me away? How could they do that? Why would they do such a thing? I remember my parents very calmly taking me in their laps and explaining that my birth parents loved me, and they wanted a better life

36

for me. They would explain, 'We don't know why you were given up for adoption. We don't know if maybe your mother was sick and couldn't take care of you, or maybe they had too many other children and not a lot of money and weren't able to take care of you.' They never expanded beyond that simple explanation. I just assumed they had or knew very little information."

The vagueness of their answer did not always sit very well with Debbie. She thought, "Why did I have to be the kid that they didn't have enough room for? I just couldn't understand."

Booth Memorial Hospital

Debbie described a time when she was about 13 years old. She was reading the newspaper and came across an article where they were interviewing the director of Booth Memorial Hospital. The article immediately caught her attention. "I knew that I had been born at Booth Memorial Hospital in Chicago. The article provided the name of the man being interviewed. In parentheses, the article said that Booth Memorial Hospital is the Salvation Army-run home for unwed mothers."

Debbie shared her reaction to the article. "All of a sudden, everything just clicked into place for me. I was able to accept for the first time that the God I had been hearing about for my whole life that loved me, that I believed in, really did care about me! He cared about where I grew up. He cared enough to put me in a home with two wonderful parents who loved unconditionally. They cared for, prayed for and nurtured me and did their best to follow God's plan for my life. This was God's plan for me from the beginning. For the first time, I remember feeling contentment and peace about being adopted and where God had put me in life."

A move to California

In the summer of 1970, Gunnar decided that maybe he was getting a little bit too old to be a full-time youth director. He felt it was time for him to go back to his first love, which was pastoring a church. Debbie recalled, "This was a very traumatic time for myself and my brother, Jeff. I would be entering my sophomore year of high school as my dad was interviewing at several different churches. Of course, Jeff, my mother and I were really pulling for the churches in the Midwest. We wanted to stay near our family and friends."

The search for a church eventually led the family to California. Debbie's father interviewed at a church in Santa Clara, California, the heart of Silicon Valley. Her father came back from the interview and sat the family down. He went on to tell them, "We just really feel that this is where the Lord wants us to be. He wants us to go to California."

Debbie remembered looking at him and saying, "Dad, are you sure God wants us to go to California? I've heard a lot of funny things about that place…and I'm not sure I want to be with those weird Californians." Despite California being known for having wonderful weather, breathtaking landscapes and beautiful beaches, it was still, according to Debbie, "worrisome to most of us from the Midwest."

In August 1970, the family moved to California. Her father began shepherding a church in Santa Clara, California. Debbie was beginning her sophomore year in high school, and Jeff was starting eighth grade. The move meant a new home, a new school, making new friends, a new church—all the other adjustments one faces when moving.

During the transition of Jeff and Debbie to new schools, Debbie's brother, Jeff, began to struggle more and more with his adoption. Debbie remembered this being a time of great turmoil for him. Jeff had a very difficult time accepting the fact that his birth parents had given him away. He struggled deeply with the thought of being rejected and abandoned despite being raised in a loving, Christian home. Jeff made a decision at that time that he was going to look for his birth parents.

Debbie remembered "Jeff's decision to search for his birth parents really hurt Mom and Dad. They were baffled and deeply saddened." Her mom and dad questioned Jeff, "We thought we have been good parents. We've loved you so much. Why isn't that enough? Why do you need to find your birth parents? What did we do wrong?"

Debbie recalled, "I remember seeing the hurt and pain on their faces. They found it difficult to understand why he was so absorbed in beginning a search for his birth parents. Prior to Jeff beginning the search for his birth parents, I'd had some curiosity about where I had come from. After seeing how much his search hurt Mom and Dad, I decided that I wasn't going to pursue any search for my own birth parents. I didn't want to add any more heartache to what they were already experiencing."

Marriage and a family

Debbie met her husband Dennis in their church's high school youth group. They began dating in her senior year of high school. Debbie graduated from high school in 1973 and immediately started college seeking her life-long dream of becoming a nurse. Dennis was a couple of years older.

He had been taking law enforcement classes in college. They dated for a couple of years. In 1975, Dennis was hired by the County of Santa Clara Sheriff's Department as a deputy. Debbie and Dennis thought it best Dennis complete the Police Academy and be off probation before they married. Debbie & Dennis married in June of 1976. They settled in a tiny duplex on the same street where Dennis grew up.

Debbie went on to say, "I was still in college after we married and worked as a nurse's aide at the county hospital. After completing college, I was hired by Santa Clara Valley Medical Center as a Registered Nurse (RN). I began my career working in a Neo-Natal Care Unit. After about year I was moved to Pediatric ICU— my life-long dream."

Their first child, Jamie

Dennis and Debbie welcomed their first child in 1979, a daughter named Jamie. Debbie vividly remembers, "As I looked into that tiny little face in the delivery room, already feeling such a strong love and bond with this baby girl. I marveled that she was the first person I had come in contact with, that shared part of the same genetic makeup as me!"

"For the first time, I thought to myself I had links to add on to my chain! Here was someone in this world that I knew looked a little bit like me. My prayer was that my little girl would grow up and enjoy some of the things that I did and act a little bit like me! It was a wonderful feeling, and at the same time, piqued my curiosity as to what this woman, my birth mother, was like. Once again, I asked myself what were the circumstances that led her to give me away to two strangers?"

"As I sat there and looked at my little baby, I felt such overwhelming love. I wondered what kind of a brave strong person did that take to be able to give her own flesh and blood, her baby, away to what she hoped would be a better home? From that point, I wanted to know more about my mother."

The Missing Piece

In 1980, Dennis and Debbie began attending Hillside Church in San Jose. Their family continued to grow with the birth of their three sons, Ryan, in 1982, Michael, in 1985 and, David, in 1988. A few months before the birth of David, a friend from church, Linda Larsen, gave Debbie a book. She knew Debbie was an avid reader and thought she needed to read this story. She also knew Debbie was adopted. Linda had just finished reading the book and thought this was an interesting story that Debbie would enjoy reading. When Linda gave Debbie the book, Linda said, "Oh, Debbie, you have GOT to read this book! It is wonderful! It's about adoption! You'll LOVE it!"

The book was titled, *The Missing Piece,* by Lee Ezell. Debbie said, "I remember not being very interested in reading it. I was wondering why do I need to read an adoption story when I had lived out my own adoption story? I could probably write my own book about it! I was convinced that I did not need to read this book! What could it possibly have to say to me?"

During her Christian walk, Debbie came to rely on her close Christian friends for insight and guidance. She observed, "We can have two types of friends. Some are believers; some are not. The non-believing friends can be good people and give us great advice and insight into some issues we might struggle with. But there is a different connection between Christian friends. C. S. Lewis once wrote, *'Is any pleasure on earth as great as a circle of Christian friends by a fire?'*[4] He also said, *'The next best thing to being wise oneself is to live in a circle of those who are.'*[5]

---

[4] *The Collected Letters of C.S. Lewis, Volume 2* (to Dom Bede Griffiths on December 21, 1941)

[5] C.S. Lewis, Hamlet: The Prince or the Poem (in *Selected Literary Essays*)

Debbie continued, "There are some unique aspects of Christian friendship, and it revolves around a spiritual connection we share as believers. God sometimes uses our friends to bring about change or new direction into our lives."

Eventually, Debbie sat down just to appease Linda and began reading the book. She read it through in one sitting! Debbie's reaction to the book was a dramatic one. "I remember some of the feelings that I felt after completing the book. After all these years, I was overwhelmed with a desire that there might possibly be a chance to meet and know who my birth parents were."

The book forced her to have some tough conversations with herself about the many conflicting feelings she felt towards her own birth mother, her parents' secrecy and her adoption. Debbie remarked, "One night while feeling completely overwhelmed by these feelings, I poured out everything to the Lord. I told Him of my deep desire to know more about my birth parents and maybe even some day meet them."

Debbie was fairly sure that at the very least her birth mother was a believer because she had chosen a Christian adoption agency to handle her adoption. She noted, "I consoled myself with the knowledge that if I couldn't meet her here on earth that at least I would meet her in heaven. I thanked the Lord again for choosing such wonderful parents for me. I told Him how much I loved and appreciated my adoptive parents, and how at the same time, I didn't want to hurt them in anyway because of this request. I ended my prayer by asking the Lord if it was His will for me to someday know my birth parents on earth, that they would first search for me. By doing that, I would know without a doubt that God was opening that door for me."

Debbie had a feeling of peace about her decision. For

the very first time, she shared openly with her husband, Dennis, the feelings she had felt all those years about being adopted. Debbie recalled those moments. "I had never really told anyone before how I felt. I shared with Dennis about how I really would like to know who my birth parents were. That night as we went to bed, we prayed. I said, God, you know I don't know much about my birth parents or where I come from. I do know that my birth mother is a Christian because we were told that much in the records that we were given by the adoption agency. So, Lord, you know that I will see them in heaven one day, and I know that too. But God, if it is part of Your plan, I would love to meet them here on this Earth."

A visit from her brother Jeff

Debbie was now at peace, and she left the future of any search or contact with her birth parents in God's hands. In July 1987, her brother, Jeff, was out visiting the family. Jeff mentioned to Dennis, "If Debbie ever wants to know anything about her birth parents, tell her to come and see me." Dennis did not make too much of the conversation. He was aware Jeff was diligently searching for himself and assumed Jeff meant using his attorney or other resources to help Debbie start a search. Dennis later shared the conversation he had with Jeff with Debbie.

Debbie also assumed that Jeff received some information from his lawyer friend on ways that she could begin searching. She didn't take it too seriously because a search was not something she felt comfortable doing. Debbie said, "I was still at peace with God opening that door in His time."

Two years later, in September 1989, Jeff was visiting the family once again. At the time, Jeff was living in Hawaii. Debbie's cousin, Linda, was also out visiting from Minnesota. Linda and Debbie had a very special relationship. They had grown up together in the Midwest. Linda had read scriptures at Debbie & Dennis' wedding and like Debbie, Linda had become a Registered Nurse. Linda lived in Minnesota but they talked on the phone every week because they were very close. Debbie described her relationship with Linda as "the sister I always wanted and more. I appreciated Linda's godly wisdom in those weekly conversations, and we grew to be best friends. My kids loved her!"

Linda was named in Debbie and Dennis's will to be the children's caretaker if something happened to them. Debbie says they often told Linda to, "just take them now!"

Debbie explained that during that visit with Jeff and Linda, they were having a nice dinner and enjoying the evening together around the table. After the kids had gone to bed, they were all sitting around talking and just catching up. For some reason, they got onto the subject of Debbie and Jeff's adoptions.

Jeff looked at Debbie and said, "I can't believe you don't want to know anything about your birth parents!" Debbie described the moment. "There was something in the sound of his voice, the expression on his face that piqued my curiosity. I knew that he knew something, and I said, "You know more than you're telling, don't you? If you know something, you better tell me!"

You'd have to know Debbie's brother, Jeff, to appreciate what he told them next. Debbie went on to describe what Jeff revealed. "He had been visiting at my parents' home in the summer of 1987 when a letter came to their house from the adoption agency that I had been adopted through. When he saw the logo of the adoption agency, he was convinced this was a letter about his search efforts. The letter was sealed so Jeff did not open it. When Mom and Dad came home that night and didn't talk about it, Jeff was determined to find that letter again."

A confirmation from God

The next day while his parents were at work, Jeff searched high and low for the letter. He finally found it in one of their bedroom dresser drawers. One can imagine his hurt, disappointment and even anger when he read it and realized that it was a letter inquiring about Debbie from her birth parents. Jeff knew he was the one who wanted to find his birth parents. It had always been so important to him. Why wasn't this letter for him? He kept his finding of the letter to himself. Even with his disappointment, he didn't want to upset the cart with his mom and dad. Secondly, he didn't think Debbie would be interested.

"Upon learning what Jeff shared, I was stunned!" Debbie recalled, "I can't tell you the kinds of emotions that were going through my head. This was the confirmation from God that I had specifically prayed for—and God answered that! I was really flabbergasted! I should not have been, but I was."

Jeff now revealed to Debbie what he had learned over two years ago—that her birth parents had actually married each other. Furthermore, Jeff told Debbie she had two full-blooded sisters! Debbie was overwhelmed, and said, "I just can't describe the feelings that were going through me when I discovered all of this new information! I felt every emotion! I was also a little bit angry with Mom and Dad. I thought we have had a really good, loving relationship for 34 years. Why couldn't my parents share this information with me?"

Several days went by, and Debbie didn't know what to do about receiving this new information. She didn't know if she should pursue this any further. She asked her cousin, Linda, for her godly wisdom. Linda encouraged Debbie and said she would be praying for her to have clarity on what the next step should be.

Debbie shares her story publicly

The following weekend, Debbie attended a women's retreat with the ladies from her home church. "Thank God for the wonderful Christian friends that He has brought to me!" Debbie said. "As I shared my story with them, they were able to put things back into God's perspective for me. Their insights helped give me wisdom as to what I should do next." Debbie noted that Proverbs 27:9 tells us:

"The heartfelt counsel of a friend is as sweet as perfume and incense." (NLT)

She observed that "Christian friends are uniquely positioned to share godly advice when we are experiencing difficult situations as well as rejoicing with us through times of answered prayer."

When Debbie told her friends about the letter Jeff found, Debbie remarked, "They shared my joy and amazement in my answered prayer! One of them commented on how fortunate I was to have had not just one but two sets of Christian parents praying for me my whole life! They validated my anger and disappointment towards Mom and Dad but would not let me wallow in those emotions."

Her friends encouraged her to be honest with her parents and tell them what she had learned. They also said to try and seek their support in any further efforts to pursue finding her birth parents. They encouraged her to write a letter to her mom and dad, expressing the love she had for them and the confusion on her part about why they did not share this information with her.

Debbie later spoke with Linda, her cousin, during their weekly phone call. Linda confirmed what Debbie's friends had said and supported whatever Debbie might do. Linda felt a letter might not clear the air and seemed a bit impersonal given Debbie's relationship with her parents. Linda suggested that Debbie meet with her parents in person. Debbie knew meeting with them would be very difficult, but it was the right course to take.

Debbie talks with her adoptive parents

After much prayer, Debbie agreed it would be better to meet with her parents instead of a letter. "I called Mom and Dad and said that we need to meet and talk." Debbie described the encounter, "It was a very difficult meeting discussing subjects we had never talked about. God taught me that they are my parents, I needed to honor them, and be loyal and reassuring to them. I was their daughter, and I was not going any place else. My place was with them, no matter what."

Debbie continued, "I let them know the many personal reasons for me wanting to learn about my birth parents and where I came from. I told them that I had never purposefully searched. I had prayed that if God wanted me to find my birth parents, He would open that door and He had."

Debbie knew it was hard for them and even a bit hurtful. However, by the end, it was a very happy meeting. Her parents gave her their support to go on and find her birth parents. In September 1989, Debbie began the long search through the adoption agency. Her initial thought was since they had already matched them up a couple of years ago, she could know next week who her birth parents were. Such was not the case.

Debbie remembers, "As I sat and waited for some information from the adoption agency, it was a very frustrating time. Patience did not come easily for me. I can remember thinking over and over, Lord, what is taking so long? You know I want to know them, and they want to know me. I've come so close. As I continued to lose patience, I remembered Psalm 139 coming to my mind over and over again. I was reminded that God had made me and knew me when I was being formed."

"For you created my inmost being; you knit me together in my mother's womb. I praise you because I am fearfully and wonderfully made; your works are wonderful, I know that full well. My frame was not hidden from you when I was made in the secret place, when I was woven together in the depths of the earth. Your eyes saw my unformed body; all the days ordained for me were written in your book before one of them came to be." (Psalm 139:13-16 NIV)

Debbie remarked, "He had written my life story before I was even born. I just needed to be patient and wait on Him."

Help from her dad

In February 1990, Debbie's father came over one night for dinner, and asked, "Have you heard anything from that adoption agency yet?"

Debbie said, "No, and I'm really frustrated."

Gunnar replied, "How about if I call and see if I can get something moving here?" This was totally unexpected. That week he called the adoption agency on Debbie's behalf.

In March 1990, Debbie's cousin Linda was again out

visiting. They had gone out to lunch, and on the way back home Linda said, "Debbie, what's going on with the adoption stuff?" Debbie said, "Oh, I just can't believe it's taking this long. I thought I would know by now." Debbie shared that her father had asked her a month earlier if there was something that he could do to expedite the process. He had called the agency to see what was going on and what was taking so long because Debbie still had not heard anything yet.

A letter from Jo Anne

Linda and Debbie pulled into the driveway, and Debbie grabbed the mail. She threw it onto the kitchen table. Out fell a letter with the letterhead from the adoption agency. Linda saw the letter and started screaming. She shouted joyously, "The Lord just wanted me to be here with you so that we could share this! I was here when you found out about it, and now I'm going to be here for the conclusion of it! This is so exciting!"

With trembling hands, Debbie tore open the letter! Out fell a picture of Dwight and Jo Anne, Debbie noting, "Two people who looked like me!" Through tears and laughter, they read every sentence eagerly. When they got to the part that said she had a sister named Debbie, she thought, "Well, at least I know they like the name!" That made her feel a little bit better.

Debbie recalled tearing up as she read. "The part that touched me the most was when I got to a portion in the letter where Jo Anne had written about when she was really depressed and kind of unsettled about what had happened. On those days, Jo Anne remembered I was always in God's hands, and she would lift me up in prayer and know that He was taking care of me."

As Debbie read the letter, she thought her life had been a rather easy one. She hadn't had any horrible struggles, and sometimes she wondered why she'd had it so good when the people around her were struggling. They were struggling to keep a faith in God, and they didn't know why they were experiencing these things. Debbie wondered, "Why am I so lucky that I've been spared so much?"

At that moment, Debbie remembered what her friends had told her when she shared her story with them. "I had two sets of Christian parents praying for me my whole life. I can't tell you how much that meant to me! It was so exciting!" Debbie could see at the end of the letter Jo Anne had apparently written their name and address. The information was covered up by white correction fluid. The adoption agency had written a short note saying, "We will be happy to put the two of you in contact with each other. However, we want you to fill out this form indicating you give your permission for the two of you to be linked together and meet if that is what you want." Debbie said, "Of course it was what I wanted!"

Iowa or California?

After 34 years of waiting, Debbie was thankful for finally getting a response. She completed the form and put it in the mail that day. When her husband, Dennis, came home from work, she showed him the letter. Debbie described what occurred after Dennis read the letter. "You have to realize that people who are in law enforcement are very curious people by nature. He was not about to sit there and look at that whited-out paper and leave it alone."

Dennis said, "I can find out what the rest of that letter says, if you want me to."

Debbie replied, "Oh, no you can't! You can't see through that whited-out part."

He said, "Sure I can." Dennis started scratching away

at the whited-out section of the letter. Dennis held it up to a light bulb and continued picking away at it. He said, "Deb, come here! I can tell you where these people live and what their names are!"

Debbie replied, "No you can't!"

Dennis announced, "Deb, you're not going to believe this. They live in California!"

Debbie objected, "No they don't! They live in Iowa!"

He insisted, "No, there's a CA at the end of this address!"

She replied, "No, it's IA! Iowa! They live in Iowa!"

Sure enough, after Dennis uncovered the names and address, they recognized the telephone area code, and found the address read "Visalia, California!"

Debbie exclaimed, "I could not believe that after all these years, God had brought us less than 200 miles of each other!" Linda was equally thrilled.

Debbie debated over the next few days whether she should call Dwight and Jo Anne. She spoke to her parents, who thought that she should wait for the approval from the adoption agency. One of Debbie's good friends told her, "Debbie, if Jo Anne and Dwight hadn't wanted you to call them, they would never have written down their number in the first place. So, I think you ought to call them."

During her weekly phone call with Linda, Debbie shared how excited she had been about the letter but still struggled with calling Dwight and JoAnne. Linda encouraged Debbie, "Deb you need to call! God put this together for a reason!"

Debbie described the moment she called. "So, with trembling hands that evening, I dialed the number from Jo Anne's letter. Just as I was dialing, I started thinking, What if Jo Anne is not home, and I have to talk to Dwight? For all these years, I had thought primarily about my birth mother. I knew I had been part of her for a whole nine months. I had not considered my birth father being in the picture. I thought, what am I going to say to him?"

Debbie speaks with Dwight

Sure enough, Dwight answered the phone. When Debbie asked for Jo Anne, Dwight told Debbie she was at choir practice. Debbie identified herself and there was a short pause on the other end of the phone. Dwight and Debbie started talking, and to Debbie's surprise, Dwight was "very easy to talk to!" They talked for about 45 minutes, and Debbie said, "We had a great time getting to know each other!" As they ended their conversation, Dwight assured Debbie that she would be receiving a phone call soon from Jo Anne.

Debbie remembered the moment vividly. "In what seemed like hours but was only about a half-hour, I received the call from my birth mother after 34 years!" Initially they were both a bit timid. There were short pauses and what sounded like a bit of tears on the other end of the phone. After a short period of time, they became more comfortable. They had a great time talking about similarities that the two of them had.

Debbie remarked, "It was such a joy to share these moments and get to know one another. If I was to rate one of the most exciting events of my life, this was certainly one of those!"

Jo Anne had earlier learned that Debbie was a nurse. Jo Anne's daughters had known Jo Anne had wanted to become a nurse. They agreed their mother would have been a great nurse. She was caring, compassionate and fascinated by all things medical—but was never encouraged to pursue her dream.

Debbie continued, "At the end of our conversation,

what touched me so much and just reinforced some of what God had done for me was that Jo Anne prayed with me! I thought, God, these are really wonderful people, and I can't believe that You are bringing them into my life!"

An invitation to get together

Debbie and Jo Anne began discussing when they would like to get together and meet each other for the first time, face to face. Jo Anne said, "As a matter of fact, Dwight has a conference up in Monterey in a little over a week, and we thought we'd like to come to San Jose and take you all out for lunch!" Monterey is about an hour away from the Bacon's home.

Debbie told Jo Anne, "I have four small children, and the thought of taking them all out to a restaurant for lunch is just a little more than I think I want to take on that day." Debbie then blurted out, "Why don't you come to my house, and I'll make you lunch?" Jo Anne quickly agreed to this invitation.

Debbie shared her mixed feelings. "After I hung up that phone, I thought, what are you doing? You are inviting these people over who you don't really know yet. You don't know what kind of food they like! What if they hate the food you make? Your house has to be cleaned! It's a disaster! Ten days is NOT enough time to repair the damage that's been done here by my four little munchkins! How are you going to make sure your kids arc going to behave themselves? You KNOW first impressions are so important! I've got to go out and get a new outfit! I've got to go on a diet! I've got to get my hair cut! And once again, HOW are you going to get those kids to behave?"

Debbie concluded, "I was a basket case for those 10 days before they came to meet us. But again, the Lord was good, and as the days got closer, I felt a real peace about our meeting!"

5.

The Reunion

On March 31, 1990, Dwight and Jo Anne drove to San Jose for the long-anticipated reunion of mother and daughter after 34 years. As they pulled up to Debbie's house, Jo Anne immediately noticed the first of several amazing similarities. Debbie's house was blue with dark blue trim—exactly the same as Jo Anne and Dwight's home.

Jo Anne remembers, "As I got out and walked up to the door, my heart was pounding because I never thought I would meet my daughter."

The door was opened by Debbie, whom Jo Anne described as "this little blonde-haired, blue-eyed young woman. I cannot tell you the feelings that I felt—the emotions that went through my heart were indescribable."

She added, "When I looked at her after all these years, I just opened my arms and she walked into them. We hugged each other and just cried as we stood there holding one another." Jo Anne looked down to see four children—her grandchildren she was meeting for the first time: Jamie, 11 years old, Ryan eight, Michael five and David, 18 months. Jo Anne noticed that Michael had red hair, and she commented, "Oh, you've got a redhead!"

Debbie replied, "Yeah, where does it come from?"

Jo Anne said, "That's easy—my mother and my brother, Bill, both have red hair." Next, Jo Anne remarked that David had dimples. Debbie said, "We (meaning neither herself nor Dennis) don't have any dimples, either!"

Jo Anne replied, "Well, my brother Bob has dimples!"

More similarities

Jo Anne and Dwight walked into the living room, and Jo Anne noticed it was decorated in "country" style—just like her own house. Debbie told her, "I have a gift for you out in the kitchen." Debbie opened up the refrigerator to give Jo Anne some flowers. They were long stem red roses with a card. Jo Anne opened the card, and it said, "Thank you for having our friend. We love her, and we look forward to meeting you!" It was signed Susan and Sandy, two good friends of Debbie Bacon.

Jo Anne noticed the dining room table and called Dwight, "Come here," she said, pointing to the table. "Look at their table."

Dwight surprisingly exclaimed, "That's the same table Debbie, (their other daughter) and Alan (her husband) have!"

Jo Anne and Dwight were astonished at the similar tastes in just about everything they observed that day—even the style of Debbie and Dennis's wedding invitation mounted on the wall which was the same style as the one given out by the other Debbie!

They sat down to talk, and over three wonderful hours,

they looked at photos and scrapbooks and filled in the gaps from 34 years of memories.

Debbie no longer felt like a "lone link on a chain." "Well, I now know who I look like and who I inherited certain traits from," she said. "With Dwight, I share my shyness and ability to turn beet red if and when anyone calls attention to me. With Jo Anne, I share a love of all things medical, along with a love of reading and music."

After their time together, Dwight was "thrilled and happy...we had a great time!" He remembers that Jo Anne was especially touched by being able to meet her grandchildren for the first time. Dwight also noticed that Debbie Bacon looked like himself, both with blonde hair and blue eyes. In regards to personality, he said she "wasn't as outgoing as Jo Anne, but she was more outgoing than me."

Even the children were well behaved. "I was impressed," Jo Anne observed. As the time came for Jo Anne and Dwight to leave, they invited Debbie and Dennis to come visit them in Visalia, so Debbie could meet her two sisters.

The sisters meet

In April 1990, Debbie Parker and Lisa were able to meet their sister and her family for the very first time. Both were very excited! Lisa remembers walking through the front door of her parent's house and seeing this woman sitting at the dining room table. "She had long blonde hair and looked like the rest of us in the family," Lisa said. "What has always amazed me is that Debbie Bacon is a full-blooded sister, not a half-sister, but a sister that is both from my mother and my father. I have always loved telling people that I have two sisters named Debbie. You can see peoples' puzzled expressions trying to figure that one out. I always tell them that my parents just liked the name Debbie. Our family loves to joke around!"

Debbie Parker remembered the day when "we went on a picnic out at Mooney Grove, a popular park in Visalia. The weather was perfect, and the food was great! We shared a little about each of us and our children. Debbie and Dennis were very friendly and easy to talk to. It was such a blessing to finally get to meet Debbie and her family. I could tell my parents were so thrilled to have the whole family together for the first time. We were all surprised how well our children got along and behaved like they had known each other for a long time. We enjoyed paddle boat rides, playing games and feeding the ducks."

Coincidence? Or God?

One evening, Dwight and Jo Anne invited their pastors, Tom and Janine Gonzalez, over for dinner. They joyfully discussed how the reunion with Debbie and her family had gone. Tom asked Jo Anne, "Did you ever find out Debbie's maiden name?"

Jo Anne replied, "Yes, I did. Her dad's name is Gunnar Hoglund."

Tom eyed Jo Anne with a knowing expression, then remarked, "Yes, and her mother's name is Doris."

Surprised, Jo Anne replied, "Yes! How did you know?"

Tom recalled, "Well, when Debbie was a little girl, I taught at the same youth camp in Illinois with her father. I knew her dad very well, and we would talk together."

Once when Debbie Bacon and family came for a visit, Tom and Janine came over for breakfast. Tom walked through the door and showed Debbie an old T-shirt with a chipmunk on it with the logo, "Camp Hickory." Debbie was amazed that she had attended the same camp where

Jo Anne's pastor had also attended! Debbie and Tom ended up talking for a long time about their camp experiences and mutual acquaintances. Another coincidence, or the hand of God?

A meeting with Debbie's parents

Earlier, Debbie had mentioned that her adoptive parents had a difficult time accepting the idea of Debbie finding out the identity of her birth parents. Sometime after the first reunion, Mr. and Mrs. Hoglund expressed a desire to meet Dwight and Jo Anne. So, the Rich's drove to San Jose to the home of Debbie and Dennis, and they all had, according to Jo Anne, a "wonderful time of visiting!" Jo Anne said, "Gunnar and Doris were a marvelous Christian couple who really love the Lord!"

Jo Anne noted, "They have done a marvelous job in raising Debbie. She has so many admirable qualities that I admire. She has wonderful self-esteem, good common sense, patience, and loves her children. But most of all, she has a love for her Lord, and I cannot tell you how much I love and admire her."

Life since the reunion

Since that wonderful reunion of families, they have all remained in close contact. Dwight observed, "It is amazing because Debbie and Dennis have fit into the family just as if Debbie would have been born into it. There is the Lord's work again because it just worked out perfectly."

Through the years the families have gotten together for holidays and special gatherings. Homemade chicken and noodles with mashed potatoes are often on the menu. Other times, the families have BBQ tri-tip steak, along with rice pilaf, and homemade vanilla ice cream with hot fudge sauce which is always a family favorite!

They have spent many hours telling stories, playing games and enjoying one another's company. They also have had their share of mishaps, such as a broken window, a trip to the emergency room for stitches and a second degree burn from a hot motorcycle engine. While camping at Pismo Beach, California, they have fond memories of watching all the kids burying themselves in the sand and rolling down the sand dunes."

The Bacon family regularly visits in Visalia, along with daughter Lisa and her husband Derek, who live in nearby Reedley. They frequently go golfing, one of Dwight's favorite pastimes. Debbie Parker and her family relocated to beautiful Lake of the Ozarks in Missouri. On several occasions, the families have been able to travel there for the annual 4th of July family reunion with Dwight's relatives from Iowa. One of the many highlights is the 4th of July fireworks show at the Parker's home.

In 2020, Jo Anne passed away. At the age of 85, she went home to be with her Lord and Savior whom she loved so much. Years after her passing, Dwight said of Jo Anne, "God is good. He gave me a wife who prayed for me every day, and I needed that. Sometimes I look around the house, and it seems like she's here—some of her knickknacks and things like the ducks…remind me of her."

Debbie Bacon's final observations

Regarding the miracle reunion and how the Lord moved in her life and in the lives of her family, Debbie made the following observations:

"I consider myself very fortunate to have grown up in the era that I did, to have the wise, loving parents that the Lord chose for me, to have suffered relatively few major traumas or difficult circumstances in my first three to four decades of my life. But since then, I have discovered that life isn't always easy. There are situations and experiences you are faced with in life that can hurt you, bring you to the brink of despair, making you feel that you are entirely alone, that God is not even there."

Debbie continued, "I know that what I learned about God during the years of discovering my birth family reassured me of how intimately God was involved in the details of my life, how much he cared for me even when I wasn't aware. I learned that He was faithful and worthy of my trust and that I could go through difficult trials and be confident that I was never alone. When God answers prayer or does something amazing in your life, you need to share it!"

Debbie emphasized, "Why do we need to share with others what God has done in our lives? We share because it increases our own understanding of the attributes of God played out in our lives. We share as a way of expressing our gratitude for God's goodness shown to us. We share as a means of publicly praising God. We share because it can bolster another believer's faith in a God who is actively involved in every aspect of our lives. We share because scripture tells us to." Psalm 107:22 says:

"Let them sacrifice thank offerings and tell of his works with songs of joy." (NIV)

Another of Debbie's favorite verses is Psalm 13:5-6:

"But I trust in your unfailing love. I will rejoice because you have rescued me. I will sing to the Lord because he is good to me." (NLT)

Debbie observed, "We share because every now and

then we need to leave our comfort zone to encourage and convince others that God has not forgotten them. Each one of you has your own story, a story filled with answered prayers and amazing ways that God has been there for you, revealed himself to you. I encourage you all to tell a friend!"

The sweater

At the Hume Lake Retreat mentioned in the Introduction, Jo Anne asked Debbie Bacon to turn the sweater inside-out to show the ragged ends which represented Jo Anne's sometimes difficult life. She then turned the sweater right-side-out, showing an intricate design on the outside of the sweater. Jo Anne commented, "This is the finished product, and the way God sees us!" Then she quoted the following verse:

"Being confident of this very thing, that he which hath begun a good work in you will perform it until the day of Jesus Christ." (Philippians 1:6 KJV)

Jo Anne concluded, "God sees our lives complete and finished. The things that happen in our lives make up our character and can be used by God to bring honor and glory to his name, or if we choose, can bring bitterness, anxiety and even inner turmoil."

Jo Anne continued, "Maybe some of you are carrying guilt, hurts and unforgiving attitudes towards yourself and others. I hope today that you'll allow God and his Spirit to minister to you."

In a message at Bayside Church in San Jose in 1997, Jo Anne also added, "Perhaps there's someone here today who has never accepted Christ, who has never opened their heart to have the assurance that if you died today, where you would go. I'd like to encourage you to ask Christ into your life. Find someone to talk to and make that commitment." She then quoted John 1:12:

"Yet to all who did receive him, to those who believed in his name, he gave the right to become children of God." (NIV)

Jo Anne finished her message by reading a poem quoted by Lee Ezell in *The Missing Piece*. Jo Anne observed, "It really is a good description of my life:"

The Weaver

My life is but a weaving between my Lord and me
I cannot choose the colors He worketh steadily
Ofttimes He weaveth sorrow, and I in foolish pride
Forget He sees the upper, and I the underside
Not till the loom is silent, and the shuttles cease to fly
Shall God unroll the canvas
and explain the reason why
The dark threads are as needful
in the weaver's skillful hand
As the threads of gold and silver
in the pattern He has planned.

—Anonymous

Photos

Left: Jo Anne at about one year old. Below: Dwight with his dogs on the farm.

Above center: Dwight's grandfather Phillip (first from left) and father, Allen, third from left, on farm in early 1900's.

Left: Jo Anne's father, Glen Donald, was owner of a Shell gas station in Mount Pleasant. He was the only employee for many years.

65

Above left: Dwight's high school graduation photo. Above right: Jo Anne's high school graduation photo. Below: Dwight and Jo Anne were married shortly before Dwight reported for active duty in the Navy.

Top: Dwight aboard a ship in the Navy. Middle left: Jo Anne's college photo. Middle center: Debbie Bacon. Middle right: Dwight's official Navy photo. Above: Jo Anne, Debbie Parker (front), Lisa (back) and Dwight.

Above: Doris, Jeff, Debbie (Bacon) and Gunnar Hoglund. Right: Evangelist Billy Graham, crusade associate Bob Denny and Gunnar Hoglund. Below left: Debbie Bacon's nursing graduation. Below middle: Debbie Bacon's daughter Jamie, Debbie B. and cousin, Linda, all three registered nurses. Below right: Debbie B. and Jo Anne.

Above: Lisa, Jo Anne, Debbie Bacon and Debbie Parker. Far left: Dwight and Jo Anne with their first great-granddaughter, Payton. Left: Dwight with Jo Anne's sweater. Below: Debbie B., Lisa, Jo Anne and Debbie P.

Above: Debbie Parker, Debbie Bacon, Jo Anne and Lee Ezell, author of "The Missing Piece," at the Hume Lake Retreat.

Left: Dwight, Debbie Bacon and Jo Anne.

Below: Front row: Jo Anne Rich, Margaret Donald (Jo Anne's mother), Debbie Bacon. Back row: Lisa Bergthold, Debbie Parker, in 1990.

Top: Derek and Lisa Bergthold, Jo Anne and Dwight Rich, Debbie and Dennis Bacon. Middle left: Lisa and Derek. Middle right: Debbie and Dennis. Bottom: Derek and Lisa Bergthold, Debbie and Dennis Bacon, Debbie and Alan Parker.

Above: Rich family grandchildren, Christmas 1993: Front: Christian Bergthold. Back row, from left: David Bacon, Aaron Bergthold, Lindsay Parker, Corey Bergthold, Ryan Bacon, Jarrett Parker, Jamie Bacon, Brittany Parker, Mike Bacon.

Left: Christmas 2023: Dwight and Jo Anne's great-grandchildren from the Bacon family. Front row: Logan Bacon, Jack Bacon, Dallas Bacon and Braden Bacon. Middle row: Presely Bacon, Zoey Issa, Payton Issa, James Bacon. Top row: Lucas Issa.

Above: A large Rich family gathering

Debbie's Letter

Hi. My name is Debbie and I am the daughter you gave up for adoption 34 years ago. I recently discovered through a series of events, that you had written my adoptive parents a letter a couple of years ago requesting information about me. My parents never showed me the letter because they were afraid it would be upsetting or difficult for me. I have to take part of the blame myself because I was never very honest with them about my feelings and desires toward you for fear of hurting them. I think they truly believed that it was unimportant to me. My adoptive parents are wonderful Christian people and the best parents anyone could ask for. I was really blessed when God put me in their home. However, I have always had strong feelings deep inside of me, even while I was growing up, about knowing you. I just never thought it would be possible.

About a year ago, I read the book "The Missing Piece". It brought up a lot of unresolved feelings I had about being adopted. As I had each one of my own kids, I experienced more and more curiosity about my own heritage. I also admired your courage and the strength it took for you to do what you had to do. I prayed at that time that God would allow me to meet you someday but if that wasn't in his plan,.I'd be content to have knowledge of you in heaven. I also prayed that if this was what He wanted, that you would first

First page of Debbie Bacon's original letter to her birth parents

73

Debbie's Letter

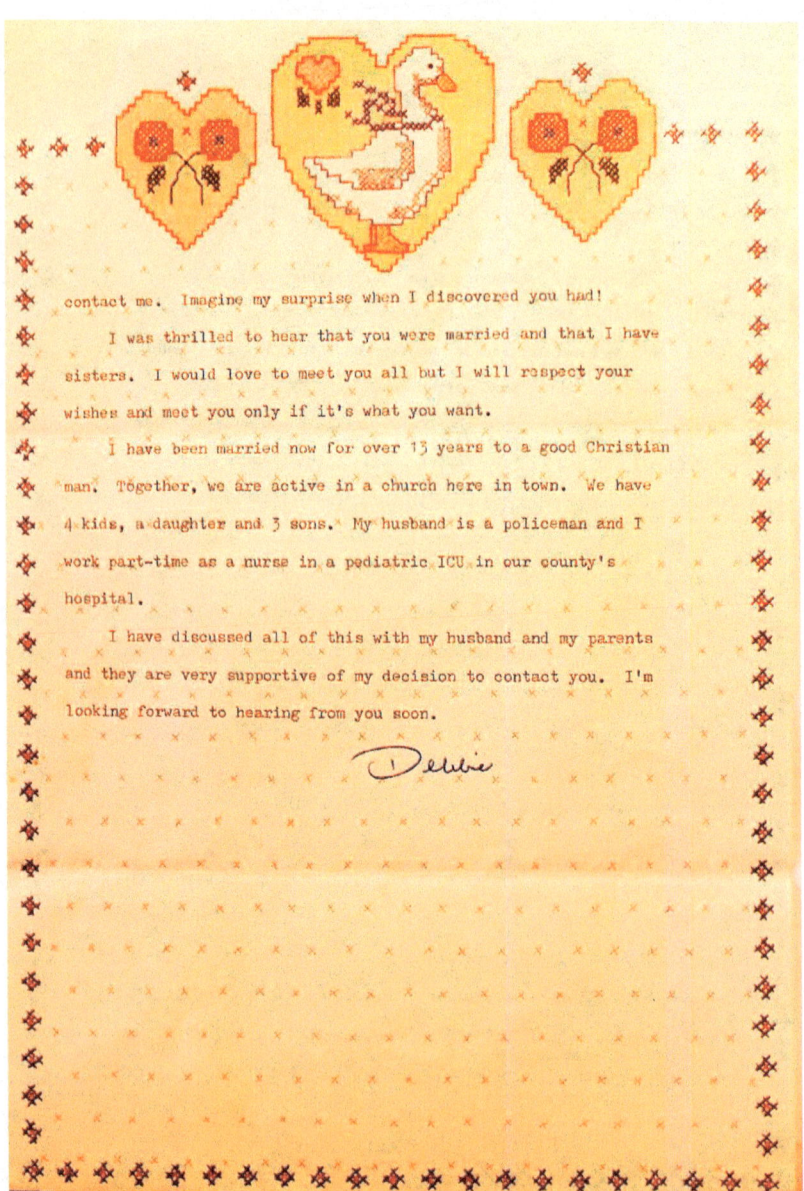

contact me. Imagine my surprise when I discovered you had!

I was thrilled to hear that you were married and that I have sisters. I would love to meet you all but I will respect your wishes and meet you only if it's what you want.

I have been married now for over 13 years to a good Christian man. Together, we are active in a church here in town. We have 4 kids, a daughter and 3 sons. My husband is a policeman and I work part-time as a nurse in a pediatric ICU in our county's hospital.

I have discussed all of this with my husband and my parents and they are very supportive of my decision to contact you. I'm looking forward to hearing from you soon.

Debbie

Second page of Debbie Bacon's original letter to her birth parents

74

6.

What can I do?

What about those who are still searching for long lost loved ones? What about those who are adopted and want to know about or meet their birth parents? What about birth parents who want to know about or meet their child given up for adoption? What do they do? Where do they go?

Fortunately, thanks to the power of the modern-day internet, there are resources available online that contain millions of times more information than what was available just a few years ago.

Here are a few suggestions to begin your search:

Find My Family Adoption Reunion Registry
https://www.findmyfamily.org/
This adoption reunion registry is for adoptees and their birth family members who are mutually searching for each other. It is for an adoptee wondering:

- How do I start looking for my birth family?
- What steps should I take to find long lost family?
- How do I find my birth mother or birth father?
- Do I have a brother or sister?
- Can a birth parent search adoption records by birthdate?
- How do I find a sibling that was given up for adoption?
- What are my origins and genealogy?
- What is my family medical history?
- How are other adoptees able to find their parents?

The Find My Family adoption reunion registry is also for biological parents who want to find the child they relinquished for adoption. Other relatives such as biological siblings and cousins also want to find the adoptee and will register the adoption search in the reunion registry.

Adopted.com
Adopted.com

Adopted.com uses a highly powerful and unique search tool that cuts across boundaries to connect you with your birth parents. By simply registering, you become part of a space that is likely shared by your biological parents.

SearchAngels.org
https://www.searchangels.org/

Performing a search to find birth family is challenging. It requires patience, zeal and a willingness to learn about new technology and search techniques that can widen the possibility of substantiating the most likely location of biological related family. Understand that our volunteers arc skilled at finding adoptee's birth family through both traditional search and genetic genealogy. We simply do not have the tools nor access to legally unseal birth records to find the children relinquished to adoption for birth parents or their siblings. If you happen to be a birth parent or sibling of an adoptee, please check their State of birth for what legal rights you might have or may currently be in legislation.

About the Author

Peter Cannon has served as a Bible study teacher, youth pastor, preacher, worship leader, mission coordinator and chaplain's assistant in jails in California's San Joaquin Valley. He is a retired teacher, former newspaper reporter and editor, filmmaker, writer and book publisher.

Acknowledgements

The author wishes to thank the following people for their help in publishing this book: Dennis Bacon, Lisa Bergthold, Debbie Parker, Dwight Rich, Debbie Bacon, Larry Gilbert, and posthumously, Jo Anne Rich.

76035006R00050